NEWARK AND REALITY

...TOGETHER AGAIN

A HARSH DOSE OF THE FUSCO BROTHERS

Also by J.C. Duffy

Meet The Fusco Brothers!

NEWARK AND REALITY
...TOGETHER AGAIN

A HARSH DOSE OF THE FUSCO BROTHERS
BY J.C. DUFFY

Andrews and McMeel
A Universal Press Syndicate Company
Kansas City

HOW ABOUT IF WE TURN OFF THE TV AND TALK ABOUT SOMETHING INTELLECTUAL FOR A CHANGE, LANCE?

LIKE WHAT?

I DON'T KNOW... HOW ABOUT KIERKEGAARD

SORRY, GLORIA, I'M NOT WEARING MY KIERKE-GUARD AT THE MOMENT....

YOU MAY WISH YOU WERE WEARING YOUR HELMET IN A MINUTE, PAL!

YOU WANT TO TURN OFF THE TV SO WE CAN TALK ABOUT KIERKEGAARD???

WHO IN THE NAME OF SOUPY SALES IS KIERKEGAARD??!!??

A WELL-KNOWN PHILOS-OPHER.

OH, YOU MEAN STEVE KIERKE-GAARD, THE BAR-TENDER AT THE DEW DROP INN?

YES, HE DOES GET OFF A GOOD ONE NOW AND THEN, I SUPPOSE....

ON SECOND THOUGHT, LET'S WATCH TV...

HOW ABOUT "MURDER, SHE WROTE"?

UH-OH, AXEL! VIEWER DISCRETION IS ADVISED!

SNAX

EETZ

ARE YOU TELLING ME THIS SHOW MAY NOT BE SUITABLE FOR ALL FAMILY MEM-BERS, AL?

BETTER SAFE THAN SORRY!!

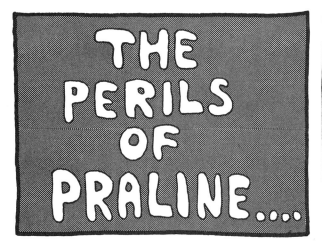

THE PERILS OF PRALINE....

14

Panel 1: WHY ARE YOU UP SO EARLY, LANCE? — KARMA. — KARMA??

Panel 2: LAST NIGHT I TURNED ON THE CLOCK....TODAY IT TURNED ON ME.

Panel 3: THAT'S PRETTY DEEP. — UNTIL I'VE HAD MY COFFEE, I'M A REGULAR KAHLIL GIBRAN.

Panel 4: WHICH RADIO STATION IS THIS, AL? — THE ONE THAT PLAYS ALL THE RELAXING MUSIC.... — BARRY MANILOW, NEIL DIAMOND, ENGELBERT HUMPERDINCK....

Panel 5: OH, THE HARD LISTENING STATION....

Panel 6: I THOUGHT THEY CALLED THIS EASY LISTENING, LANCE.... — FOR YOU, EASY... FOR ME, DIFFICULT!

Panel 7: HI, GLORIA! WHAT ARE YOU DOING?

Panel 8: OH...GEE, I REALLY WANTED TO SEE YOU.... — COULDN'T YOU JUST DO THAT OVER HERE?

Panel 9: WELL, YES, IT WOULD BE SILLY TO CART YOUR DIRTY DISHES OVER HERE! — THAT'S RIDICULOUS!!

Panel 10: I MEANT YOU COULD DO MY DISHES OVER HERE.... — HELLO? — HELLO??

17

21

22

"THE AIR WAS THICK WITH A RANCID PANIC, AS THE BURLY RUFFIAN CLOSED THE DOOR BEHIND ME..."

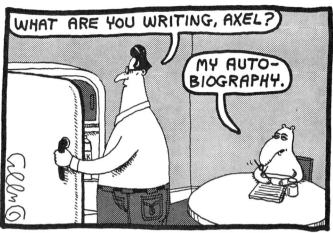

WHAT ARE YOU WRITING, AXEL?

MY AUTOBIOGRAPHY.

OH, I HEARD ABOUT THAT... "I WAS A TEEN-AGE WOLVERINE"?

RIGHT.

MY LIFE'S BEEN A RICH, EXCITING TAPESTRY, LANCE, AND I THOUGHT I SHOULD GET IT ALL DOWN BEFORE IT SLIPPED MY MIND.

HOW'S IT COMING?

I'M UP TO THE PART WHERE YOU LOCKED ME IN THE CLOSET FOR SPILLING MY CEREAL.

WHAT?!!? I NEVER—

SEE THIS SALAMI?

IT MAKES FOR A GOOD READ.

IT MAKES FOR A GOOD PUMMEL!

WHO WAS THAT ON THE PHONE, RÖLF?

MISS WRIGHT.

MISS RIGHT? WOW, THAT'S GREAT! YOU FINALLY MET MISS RIGHT!

WE'VE NEVER MET.

HOW ROMANTIC! LOVE AT FIRST SOUND! HAVE YOU SET A DATE?

SHE SET ONE... THE 13TH.

GREAT! I'LL START CALLING PEOPLE!

DON'T PLAN ON CALLING ANYBODY AFTER THE 13TH, AL— THAT'S WHEN MISS WRIGHT SAYS SHE'LL SHUT OFF THE PHONE IF WE DON'T PAY THE BILL.

LANCE! THERE'S A GIGANTIC COCKROACH IN THE BATHTUB!!

DID YOU WANT TO TAKE A BATH?

THE BIGFOOT DIET

HOMEOWNER REVEALS: "ELVIS ATE MY HOUSE!"

WILD NEWS

NO, BUT I THOUGHT MAYBE SOMEBODY SHOULD TAKE CARE OF IT... SOME ADULT... SOMEBODY BIG... SOMEBODY BRAVE....

YOU'RE RIGHT, AXEL... I'LL PHONE GLORIA.

PARDON ME, MISS—WHAT TIME DO YOU HAVE?

GO, AL!

I HAVE ALL THE TIME IN THE WORLD, BIG GUY....

YOU'RE VERY FORTUNATE.

AL—I THINK SHE'S INTERESTED...

INTERESTED? IN WHAT?

IN MAKING A LITTLE TIME...

TIME IS THE LAST THING SHE NEEDS, LARS! PAY AT-TENTION!!

I GUESS I JUST CAN'T READ WOMEN LIKE YOU CAN, AL....

35

38

ATTRACTIVE OUTFIT, AL...VERY AMISH....

CREEPY TALES!

I UNDERSTAND THE AMISH ARE KNOWN AS "THE PLANE PEOPLE"...I THOUGHT IT MIGHT BE NICE TO LOOK LIKE I'M PART OF THE JET SET.

I BELIEVE THAT'S "PLAIN", AL, AS IN NOT FANCY...YOU LOOK LIKE YOU'RE PART OF THE NOT-FANCY SET....

OH...WELL, IT'S A BEGINNING.

OOH-LET'S WATCH DOLLY PARTON ON THE TONIGHT SHOW! I'M A BIG ADMIRER OF HER TALENTS....

TALENTS? PLURAL?

BOTH BARRELS!

I'M GROWING TIRED OF YOUR DOUBLE-ENTENDRES, LANCE.

WELL THEN, GLORIA, YOU'LL BE HAPPY TO KNOW THAT I'M CLOSE TO PERFECTING THE QUADRUPLE-ENTENDRE!

BARRING ANY LABORATORY EXPLOSIONS OR PATENT OFFICE RED TAPE, I SHOULD BE MAKING AN ANNOUNCEMENT SOON.

YOU CALL THIS COFFEE, LANCE? THIS ISN'T COFFEE... YOU SHOULD BE ASHAMED TO CALL THIS COFFEE!

DID I CALL IT COFFEE?

WELL, NO....

I WOULD BE ASHAMED TO CALL IT COFFEE IF I HAD TRIED TO MAKE COFFEE...AS IT IS, I GUESS I SHOULD BE PROUD THAT YOU EVEN THINK IT'S COFFEE... "COFFEE" IS A COMPLIMENT, CONSIDERING WHAT IT ACTUALLY IS! IF YOU ONLY KNEW....

NEVER MIND-LET'S JUST CALL IT BAD COFFEE.

LET'S CALL IT GREAT COFFEE.

HOW ABOUT OKAY COFFEE?

DEAL.

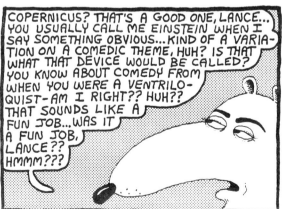

41

43

WELL, LANCE, WHAT DO YOU SAY?

WELL, ON THE ONE HAND, GLORIA, I'M NOT REALLY INTERESTED IN MOVING YOUR AIR CONDITIONER RIGHT NOW...

YEAH....

BUT ON THE OTHER HAND, I'M NOT REALLY INTERESTED IN HEARING YOU COMPLAIN ABOUT IT ALL NIGHT...

YEAH....

SO I GUESS, ETHICALLY, I SHOULD JUST DISQUALIFY MYSELF FROM THE ENTIRE CONTROVERSY...

WHY IS THAT??

I HAVE A CONFLICT OF DISINTEREST

TAKING AXEL FOR A WALK, RÖLF?

DON'T PUSH ME, LANCE! NO ONE IS "TAKING" ANYBODY FOR A WALK! AND IF YOU SAY ANYTHING LIKE "DON'T FORGET THE LEASH," THERE COULD BE DIRE CONSEQUENCES!

RELAX, AXEL—I REALIZE YOU'RE FAR TOO MATURE FOR A LEASH... DON'T FORGET THE POOPER-SCOOPER, RÖLF.

HEY—SLEEPING BEAUTY! HOW ABOUT LETTING SOMEBODY ELSE SIT ON THE COUCH?!?

THE DOCTOR SAYS HE CAN'T BE MOVED, AXEL.

HIS DOCTOR SAYS HE'S TOO SICK TO BE MOVED??

NO, MY DOCTOR SAYS HE'S TOO HEAVY FOR ME TO MOVE HIM.

WHAT ARE YOU DOING, AL?

I'M CHECKING YOUR TEENAGE RECORD COLLECTION FOR SATANIC MESSAGES, AXEL.

I SEE... FIND ANYTHING?

WELL, WHEN YOU PLAY THIS GUY MOZART BACKWARD, IT SOUNDS LIKE HE'S SAYING "TURN ME ON, BEELZEBUB"!...

AL-THAT'S AN INSTRUMENTAL ALBUM...THERE ARE NO WORDS ON IT-BACKWARD, FORWARD OR SIDEWAYS!

OH...MAYBE YOUR TURN-TABLE HAS A FAULTY CAR-TRIDGE....

MAYBE YOU'RE THE ONE WITH THE FAULTY CARTRIDGE, AL!

HOW DOES YOUR FORK EVER LOCATE THAT TINY LITTLE PLACE YOU CALL YOUR MOUTH, LANCE?

I GUESS COMPARED TO THAT GRAND CANYON OF YOURS, MY MOUTH WOULD SEEM SMALL, AXEL...

BUT ALSO, THIS FORK IS EQUIPPED WITH A SOPHISTICATED HEAT-SEEKING DEVICE, AND IS AUTOMATICALLY DRAWN TO THE WARMEST SPOT ON MY FACE- MY RED-HOT LOVERBOY LIPS!

THERE GOES MY APPETITE!

I'M REALLY SICK OF HEARING THE MUSIC OF MY YOUTH BEING USED IN COMMERCIALS!

WELL, AT LEAST THEY'RE SELLING A LUXURY CAR....

"COME ON AND LET THE GOOD TIMES ROLL!"

NO, THE WOMAN IN THE LUXURY CAR IS SPEEDING TO THE SUPERMARKET FOR SOME LUXURY TOILET PAPER!

!#%©!!✭✲!!

HEY, KID—HOW IN THE NAME OF BETTY CROCKER IS A PERSON SUPPOSED TO REACH THE STUFF ON THE TOP SHELF?

WHY DON'T YOU TRY THIS SPECIALLY DESIGNED TOILET PAPER GRABBER, MISTER?

GEE, WHAT WILL THEY THINK OF NEXT?

PERSONALLY, I THINK USING ONE OF THESE IS LIKE USING A BRIDGE WHEN PLAYING POOL...IT'S FOR WIMPS.

FOR YOUR INFORMATION, JUNIOR, I WAS REACHING FOR COFFEE, WHICH I TAKE VERY STRONG! I THINK TOILET PAPER IS FOR WIMPS!

46

I THINK I'M GETTING A TOOTHACHE, LANCE...I HOPE THE DENTIST DOESN'T WANT TO PULL IT! I'M SCARED!!

DON'T WORRY, AL—THEY REALLY DO THEIR BEST TO AVOID PULLING A TOOTH.

THAT'S REASSURING...IS THAT BECAUSE IT CAN WEAKEN THE SURROUNDING TEETH?

NO, IT'S BECAUSE THEN THEY HAVE ONE LESS TOOTH TO GO ON FILLING FOR YEARS AND YEARS.

I FEEL BETTER.

CAN I BORROW A STAMP, RÖLF?

POSTAGE?

NO, IT'S YOUR STAMP OF APPROVAL I CRAVE.

NEVER MIX IN SARCASM WITH BEGGING, LANCE—IT'S A BASIC RULE OF THUMB.

HOW ABOUT THE RULE OF THUMB WHERE I BEND YOURS BACK UNTIL WE HEAR A LOUD CRUNCHING SOUND?

THREATS AND BEGGING—NOW THERE'S A COMBINATION THAT WORKS!

THANK YOU SO MUCH.

AH-CHOO!!

GESUNDHEIT.

BOY, THAT WAS SOME GOOD SNEEZE! WHAT A SENSUAL SNEEZE THAT WAS! MY NOSE IS ALL TINGLY, I'M LIGHTHEADED—WOW! LET ME JUST BASK IN THE AFTERGLOW!!

YOU'RE VERY LONELY, AREN'T YOU, AL?

THAT MUST BE IT.

I REALLY HAVE TO QUIT WATCHING THAT RIDICULOUS SOAP OPERA! IT'S GIVING ME A TWISTED VIEW OF REALITY!

TIME
THE CRISIS CRISIS

WHICH ONE IS IT—"THE YOUNG AND THE RESTLESS"? "THE BOLD AND THE BEAUTIFUL"?

"THE LANCE AND THE GLORIA."

HOW WAS YOUR DATE, LARS?

NOT GREAT...

HER CAR BROKE DOWN UP ON LOOKOUT HILL...I TRIED TO SEE WHAT I COULD DO, BUT I COULDN'T GET HER DISTRIBUTOR CAP OFF....

I DIDN'T KNOW WOMEN STILL WORE DISTRIBUTOR CAPS.

ARE YOU JUST WAKING UP, LANCE? IT'S 2:17PM!

THANK YOU, BIG BEN.

WHAT KIND OF EXAMPLE IS THIS TO BE SETTING FOR AN IMPRESSIONABLE TEEN?!?

THAT WOULD BE ME.

SEE IT AS A LESSON IN PERSONAL HYGIENE, RÖLF... BY GETTING UP IN THE AFTERNOON, I COMPLETELY AVOID THE DANGER OF MORNING BREATH.

MAKES SENSE, ACTUALLY....

67

79

TIME TO EAT THE DONUTS....

I'M OFF TO DINKY DONUTS, LANCE...WANT ANYTHING?

I THOUGHT NORMA WORKED THE NIGHT SHIFT, RÖLF.

SHE DOES... LURLENE WORKS THE DAY SHIFT.

LURLENE? LOVELY NAME... ISN'T IT FROM THE LATIN, MEANING "CRULLER PROVIDER"?

RIGHT.

SO, IS LURLENE SOMEBODY NEW?

NEW, VIBRANT, AND SHE HAS SOMETHING NORMA DOESN'T HAVE...

WHAT'S THAT?

GLAZED BUNS.

SOUNDS FETCHING...

IT'S REALLY AMAZING WHAT THEY CAN DO WITH COS-METIC SURGERY THESE DAYS...

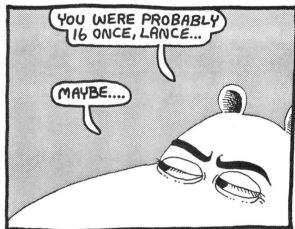

BOY, I FEEL GREAT TODAY! I FEEL LIKE THE WORLD IS MY OYSTER! KNOW WHAT I MEAN??

WELL, I DON'T LIKE OYSTERS, SO IT PROBABLY WOULDN'T BE THE SAME THRILL FOR ME...

I ONCE WOKE UP FEELING LIKE AMERICA WAS MY DONUT, BUT THAT'S ABOUT IT.

THAT'S PATHETIC, AL.

NOT REALLY, LARS... I USUALLY WAKE UP FEELING LIKE NEW JERSEY IS MY PITTED PRUNE... NOW THAT'S PATHETIC!

I STAND CORRECTED.

WHAT HAVE YOU GOT FOR A HEADACHE, GLORIA?

HOW ABOUT A SERIOUS, IN-DEPTH DISCUSSION ABOUT OUR RELATIONSHIP? THAT USUALLY GIVES YOU A HEADACHE, LANCE.

THAT SOUNDS GREAT, BUT I DON'T HAVE TIME FOR AN IN-DEPTH DISCUSSION RIGHT NOW...HOW ABOUT JUST A QUICK TIRADE OR A FAST HARANGUE?

I CAN'T GUARANTEE YOU A HEADACHE....

A MAALOX MOMENT WILL BE FINE.

I CAN'T SEEM TO LOCATE MY OTHER SLIPPER, AXEL... MIGHT YOU KNOW WHERE IT IS?

WHY WOULD YOU THINK I WOULD KNOW WHERE YOUR STUPID SLIPPER IS, LANCE?

I THOUGHT MAYBE YOU HAD THE PRIMAL URGE TO BURY SOMETHING IN THE BACK YARD.

IT'S THE PRIMAL URGE TO BURY YOU IN THE BACK YARD THAT HAS ME WORRIED...

WORRIED THAT YOUR TRUE SAVAGE NATURE WILL BE REVEALED?

WORRIED THAT YOU'RE TOO HEAVY TO CARRY OUT TO THE BACK YARD.

YOU KNOW WHAT YOUR PROBLEM IS, LANCE? YOU'RE JUST A BIG JERK! I DON'T KNOW WHY I THOUGHT IT WAS MORE COMPLICATED THAN THAT....

OH, YEAH??

I HATE TO INTERRUPT YOU NUTTY LOVESICK KIDS, LANCE, ESPECIALLY RIGHT BEFORE YOUR SNAPPY COMEBACK, BUT AS YOU KNOW, THIS IS "AXEL WEEK"!

WHAT THE HECK IS "AXEL WEEK"??

IT'S THE FORMERLY STUPID, NOW SUDDENLY SMART IDEA IN WHICH HE GETS TO HOG THE LIMELIGHT FOR A WEEK... MY APOLOGIES FOR POOH-POOHING IT EARLIER, AXEL.

AH...A SOLITARY WALK IN THE PARK DURING "AXEL WEEK"! NOBODY AROUND TO BLOCK THE NATURAL FLOW OF MY CREATIVE JUICES... WHAT A TREAT!

A SOULFUL CLOSEUP OF MY EYES WOULD PROBABLY BE EFFECTIVE RIGHT ABOUT NOW....

HEY! WHAT ARE YOU DOING HERE?!!?

I THOUGHT SOMEBODY SHOULD KEEP AN EYE ON YOU IN THIS PARK BECAUSE OF RECENT REPORTS OF A MONSTER STALKING IT...

WHAT KIND OF A MONSTER?

THE DREADED CLOVEN-HOOFED EGOMANIAC.

VERY FUNNY, LARS...

BUT I'M NOT CLOVEN-HOOFED.

THEY WERE PANICKY REPORTS.

AL! WHERE HAVE YOU BEEN? YOU MISSED "AXEL WEEK"!!

"AXEL WEEK"?

YES! MY LAWYER GOT ME A PROVISION IN MY CONTRACT WHERE I GET FEATURED IN THE STRIP EVERY DAY FOR A WEEK!!

GEE...I SHOULD HAVE HIRED A LAWYER INSTEAD OF A STUPID PUBLIC RELATIONS FIRM! THEN I COULD SKIP THESE EXHAUSTING PROMOTIONAL TRIPS TO FRANCE BECAUSE THEY CONSIDER ME A GENIUS! NOW I KNOW HOW JERRY LEWIS FEELS!!

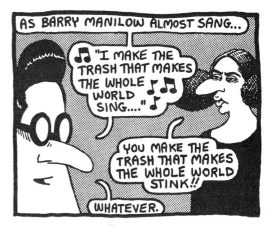

LANCE, I'M GETTING TIRED OF WATCHING YOUR JAW DROP TO THE FLOOR EVERY TIME A HOT BABE WALKS TO THE LADIES' ROOM!

AND I'M GETTING TIRED OF THE WAY YOU DISTORT THE FACTS JUST TO SUPPORT YOUR DELUSIONAL IDEAS, GLORIA!

LIKE WHAT FACTS?

LIKE THE FACT THAT SOME OF THEM HAVE BEEN WALKING TO THE SALAD BAR!!

I'D LIKE TO TAKE BACK WHAT I SAID ABOUT YOU DROPPING YOUR JAW TO THE FLOOR EVERY TIME AN ATTRACTIVE WOMAN WALKS BY, LANCE... I WAS WRONG.

THANK YOU, GLORIA... YOU REALIZED I DON'T HAVE A LASCIVIOUS MIND?

I REALIZED YOU DON'T HAVE A JAW.

HOW ABOUT GOING TO THE STORE FOR ME, AXEL?

SLOTH LOUNGING IN THE 90'S

YOU KNOW, IT'S FUNNY, LANCE— I WOULD GO TO THE ENDS OF THE EARTH BECAUSE OF YOU, BUT I WON'T GO TO THE CORNER STORE FOR YOU...PRETTY IRONIC, HUH?

WHAT IF I WERE TO GRASP YOUR NECK THE WAY I GRASP THAT SUBTLE DISTINCTION?

I'D REMIND YOU THAT STRANGLING CUTE LITTLE ANIMALS IN FAMILY NEWSPAPERS IS NO WAY TO WIN A PULITZER.

RIGHT NOW I'D SETTLE FOR A HOWITZER!

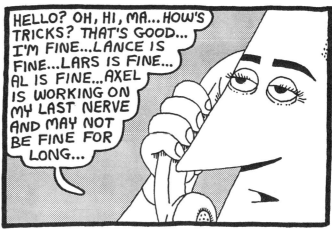

A. THE SERIOUS BRAIN TEASER...

B. THE SERIOUSLY BRAIN-TEASED.

OUCH!!

WHAT'S THE MATTER, AL—IS THAT CROSSWORD HURTING YOUR BRAIN?

THIS IS A NOTORIOUSLY DIFFICULT CROSSWORD, RÖLF! BUT I BELIEVE THAT WITHOUT STRENUOUS EXERCISE THE BRAIN BECOMES FLABBY...

NO PAIN, NO GAIN!

I GUESS THE LAST THING YOU NEED IS CELLULITE ON YOUR CEREBELLUM....

EXACTLY!

SO WHICH CROSSWORD IS IT—THE NEW YORK TIMES?

I WISH...

NO, I'M WAY PAST THE GENERAL KNOWLEDGE ONES AT THIS POINT...I'M CURRENTLY EXPLORING CROSSWORDS FROM SPECIAL INTEREST MAGAZINES...

LIKE WHAT?

TV GUIDE.

124

LANCE FUSCO
RÖLF FUSCO
LARS FUSCO
* AL FUSCO
AXEL FUSCO

WHY DO YOU HAVE AN ASTERISK NEXT TO YOUR NAME ON THE DOORBELL, AL?

IS THAT WHAT THAT'S CALLED?

YES...WHAT DOES IT MEAN?

THE SAME THING IT MEANS ON A RESTAURANT MENU.

WHICH IS?

IT INDICATES "HOT AND SPICY."

AH, ONCE AGAIN IT'S SPRING... TIME TO START SHINING UP THE CLUBS!

I KNOW WE'VE HAD OUR DIFFERENCES, LANCE—BUT VIOLENCE?!?

I MEANT GOLF CLUBS, AXEL!!

OH...I DON'T DO GOLF—I'M NOT TALL ENOUGH.

WHAT ABOUT MINIATURE GOLF?

I'M NOT STUPID ENOUGH.

HI, RÖLF! GUESS WHAT'S IN THE BOX!

THE HEAD OF ALFREDO GARCIA?

A CD PLAYER!

THIS END UP

FRAGILE

I WON IT IN A RAFFLE AT DINKY DONUTS! WELCOME TO THE 21ST CENTURY!

DON'T YOU MEAN WELCOME TO THE 1990S LARS?

YES AND NO... I DON'T SEE US AFFORDING ANY ACTUAL CDS UNTIL THE 21ST CENTURY.